# Rest

# Rest

## Margaree Little

Four Way Books
Tribeca

Library of Congress Cataloging-in-Publication Data

Names: Little, Margaree, author.
Title: Rest / Margaree Little.
Other titles: Poems. Selections
Description: New York, NY : Four Way Books, [2018] | Includes bibliographical references.
Identifiers: LCCN 2017029368 | ISBN 9781945588105 (softcover : acid-free paper)
Classification: LCC PS3612.I8758 A6 2018 | DDC 811/.6--dc23
LC record available at https://lccn.loc.gov/2017029368

This book is manufactured in the United States of America and printed on acid-free paper.

Four Way Books is a not-for-profit literary press. We are grateful for the assistance we receive from individual donors, public arts agencies, and private foundations.

This publication is made possible with public funds from the National Endowment for the Arts.

PROUD MEMBER

We are a proud member of the Community of Literary Magazines and Presses.

Distributed by University Press of New England
One Court Street, Lebanon, NH 03766

For the person we found, whose real name is known by those who loved him

What if it is rest and nothing else that

we want? Is it a findable thing, small?
In what hole is it hidden? Is it, maybe,
a country? Will a guide be required who
will say to us how?

—Carl Phillips

Contents

I.

The Visit  3

Map  6

The Calling  9

What Was Missing  11

Rest  13

What Begins as a List of Things Lost to Him  15

The Subjunctive  16

Revision  18

Vigil  20

The Dead  22

II.

*List of Recovered Human Remains, Arizona-Mexico Border, 2009-2010*

The Orchard  28

February  31

The Mattress  31

What Was Missing (2)  32

Omission  34

The Field  35

Harvest  37

Pace  39

The Instrument Maker  40

The Spring  42

Return  43

III.

*List of Recovered Human Remains, 2009-2010, continued*

Rest (2)   50

Remainder   52

The Heron   53

Using It   56

The Familiar   58

At Trustom Pond   60

The Shirt   62

The Spool   63

The Studio   64

Cairns   67

Thanksgiving   69

*List of Recovered Human Remains, 2009-2010, continued*

Notes

I.

# THE VISIT

*You should get out of here,* my friend said, so we drove north

out of Arizona, and coming up through California the shape we saw by the road

was not a person, the green we saw not the green

of the Border Patrol's *dogcatcher trucks,* that's what they call them,

cage in the back so from the back you can see

the desert running north as they drive south, Red-tailed Hawks

taking off in the heat, the heat like another person—this green

was the green of fields north of Los Angeles, Pacific green

opening to our left as we drove, green eyes

of my friend's oldest sister, who showed us the way

into the forests of Santa Cruz, where men from Portugal used to cut

Redwood trees to burn, and built kilns from stones they broke with other stones, and dropped the limestone from the hills into the kilns, and kept it there,

and stayed by it, and added wood all night to it, so in the kilns

it became another thing, the men coming back to town,

two days off after two weeks in the forest,

moths around the lamps, trains calling out in the night,

dragging the stone north. It's heavy,

that stone. But they carried it. And men built San Francisco out of it,

and they didn't complain, I think, as my friend didn't complain or swear like I did

when the two of us carried the body, Elias—

and the stone didn't burn when San Francisco burned in 1906,

my friend's oldest sister tells me this in her family's house in Santa Cruz,

she's sitting at the piano to play us sonatas,

she's making us coffee, she's making us bread, she's cutting pieces of apples

into our hands, as though she didn't know where our hands had been.

# MAP

Stupid mind, turning away from music and saying there is no music. North Carolina in January, snow on the river, my teacher is saying, *It's like walking on a tightrope*, my teacher is saying, *Don't look down.*

\*

From Tucson take 19 south to Arivaca. Turn on Ruby Road.

The February sun is white behind John, who's Quaker and who invited Annie and me out for milkshakes when he heard. He's saying, *Everyone dies*, and I say, *This is different*, meaning the geopolitical facts whereby some people have to leave home and other people can stay, and the only way to cross is through the desert. He says, *Different how?* and I say, *He was killed*, and Annie puts her head on my shoulder.

\*

Pass Ruby, the ghost town, the pilings from the mine.

At the training in September they'd explained: a typical sign of heat sickness is confusion. Sometimes the skin becomes sensitive, the softest cloth an irritant. Sometimes people are found with their clothes next to them, folded neatly.

*

Park on the road just in from waypoint 1186, or on Ruby Road, at 1177, near mile marker 12. Hike south.

We're hanging silver stars and tinsel from the roof of the shelter, since it's Advent, we're making cupcakes, drinking Coke, when Jorge comes in, Jorge who keeps crossing and then showing up again, who wears a shark tooth necklace he got when he lived in LA. This time his face is gray and his hands are shaking. I sit across from him and he tells me about the teenage girl they found in what used to be a river, how he sat all night by her, how he walked all the way back here in the morning.

Waypoint 3831 is what you want to aim for.

*

*Maybe it's time to give him over into the care of God,* my friend says on the phone. I try to picture *Care of God*—

And remember how she played *Swing Low, Sweet Chariot* on the piano, while the rest of us tried to translate *chariot*—

At the gate in the fence, cross the fence and head downhill, and cross the
small canyon. On the far side of the canyon, head uphill for the trail—

Or Kevin saying, *You don't have to watch*—

Or El Paso in the evening, a storm coming up or leaving, the sky dark
and the wind in everything where I am walking by the storefronts along
the border close to the bridge to Juárez, and one storefront is blue, white
lettering on the front that says *Estrella*, light coming out of everything like
it's taking care of you, and I go into a market across the street to buy pears
and fish I'll eat in the hotel for dinner, and coming out the sky is already
darker, the blue of the building across the street already a different color.

\*

After 3831 go down the steep hill to 3855. This is the part that's hard to go
down. Take the trail that runs above the wash, to the spot where the trails
fork, Annie saying, *I feel numb*, I'm saying, *Don't forget to come back.*

Then rain in the morning, rain in the weeks after that.

# THE CALLING

Because three Sisters work here, one named *Engracia* which means *full of grace*, here at the shelter where people come with blisters and red eyes after walking through the desert and being driven back again,

because I am reading Sophocles, how he writes, *That was indeed a great / inaugural time of sorrows*, and what I see is *inaugural*,

and there are horses on the hills above the apartment building where I stay,

and I am teaching the Sisters English and Engracia laughs when she tries to speak. She tells me about *saber* and *conocer*, the verbs that mean *to know* and *to be familiar with*, that have two different meanings,

and in the evening piano music from a radio comes down the steps and I go up in a black dress through the yellow light to give the lesson. Engracia asks, *and you, what are you looking for?*

and tells me a story about Samuel and Eli, *Eli*, variant form of *Elias*, meaning *Lord my God*, how Samuel was a boy and a servant to Eli, and at night Samuel heard someone call his name, and went out to Eli, thinking it was Eli calling, but Eli said *go lie down*

and the third time Eli said, *it must be God, when you hear it again, come out and say, Speak your servant hears you*—

*I'm coming back here to stay* is what I write to my friend,

and later read the rest, how the message God gave Samuel was that Eli would be killed, and all his sons, and Samuel gave the message to Eli, *and Samuel grew, and the Lord was with him, and let none of his words fall to the ground.*

# WHAT WAS MISSING

The undersides
of the hands. The hair.

The eyes. The chin,
the spot where the chin

becomes the neck.
Both of the arms.

The armpits.
The left tennis sneaker,

Wilson brand.
Water that we could

have left for him.
The sound of trains.

The canals that carry sound
into the ears. The ears.

Bruises and lips.
Wallet, if there ever was

a wallet. Light after a while.
Dark after a while.

Thighs. A name.
The face, the neck.

# REST

*for Marianne Boruch*

By a Chicago lake, in a Chicago summer,
1962 or 63, and she twelve or thirteen,
I think, she'd only said that she was young,

she spent the summer with a group of girls,
sleeping in tents, studying
different kinds of pines—

White Pine, for example, five needles
in each bundle, one needle
for each letter in its name—

and from June to September, she said, they kept
the same fire going, each girl learning
when it needed dry wood or green wood—

no one could leave that spot by the lake for long.
She would understand
how my friends and I carried the man we found

together, the forty pounds of him
inside the white bag the sheriff brought,
the white of the bag showing the way

through the dark. And the mountains,
the thin grass in the desert
like hair that had fallen out

and then like grass, Border Patrol trucks
on the far side of the mountains,
their light coming to meet his light.

# WHAT BEGINS AS A LIST OF THINGS
## LOST TO HIM

Hands getting cold at night. Light flashing
through the chain-link fence on the bridge
over the dammed river from El Paso, sun getting low

in the West so the light comes fast between the shadows.
And Betty's minestrone soup and Peter's bread
in their house in Juárez, and outside in Juárez

the sound of dogs barking. And the evening, and the fish
the woman next door fries when Betty and I visit,
and the woman's daughter, Selia, who is seventeen—

Age, is that lost? Lost, the idea of seventeen?—
Selia, who has two braids tied with different-colored
rubber bands, one red, one blue, her hair

dyed the soft red of carnations.
Lost, the feeling of shame, of shyness?
What about the feeling of being far from home?

And Betty's hands on my hands in their yard at night,
and the sky in the morning above Selia's street
like a field of lemon trees, just as pale, just as simple.

# THE SUBJUNCTIVE

If not the cane fields, if that's not where he worked,
it could have been a city with white walls and gray birds
in the plaza, children begging on the steps

of the church. Or maybe he came from the mountains
in the south, sound of crickets at night,
smell each day of each day's fire. And he loved the sound

of one woman's voice, or the underside
of her wrists. And their son cried, and their son
was hungry. And he undid the laces on his shoes

before he lay down here. Or he walked in circles first,
underneath the stars and moon, certain that this way, yes,
this way was north. Or his hands swelled

in the heat. Certainly, his hands swelled.
Or he folded his hands under his head, told himself he'd stop
for just a few minutes, just to rest. And it was August,

I know that it was August, because the sheriff said
it had been six months at least, time to be buried by the shale
and then unburied, soft wind giving him new names,

or he went back home, or he never left home,
he didn't try to cross, never put his mouth
to the gravel here, never thought that it was water.

# REVISION

Water, this is the first revision, that we brought water for him in time

No, that he'd had it himself, he carried a river on his back and drank from it that whole walk through the desert, and we only found his body because he'd decided to leave it behind

Because he was an angel, briefly inhabiting a body on earth, so there is no one to miss him, no one with bloodshot eyes waking up every day to *Where is he where is he is he alive*, the wind moving the blades of the old fan around in the window

He was a gift to the bees and birds and little bats that come through Arizona in the spring, little bats, one on each of his fingers

Third revision, he still has fingers

And the part about the sheriff and the men he brought, they were just boys, let them forget how they threw the bag of him up on the rocks

And the white flowers blossoming in the city now in April, make them stop

A doctor walked that wash three weeks ago and tells me that she found more bones, she found a jaw, and there was already a jaw, so include this, too, that it was not one man there, but two, that is, one man and a jaw

My mother says some trees in Kingston are turning green now with the early heat, but others answer only to the length of days

Do we have to keep the following: panic, thirst

And the stars overhead like white women

# VIGIL

Warm night in the city, dogs barking as a train goes past,
the Catalina Mountains dark behind me

and in front a house, friends. Tomorrow we'll go back
to the spot where we found the man, so tonight

we plan, my friends and I, what we'll burn there,
what we'll build. Wendy says she'll bring herbs—

cedar, sage, licorice root, little yellow flowers, things to help
the soul get clean. And we'll use stones

to build an altar there. And Annie will bring candles,
she says, the tall kind of candles they sell in grocery stores

all over the city, *vigil candles*, they're called,
because they burn so long. We'll light them on the rocks,

stay awhile in the wash, in that low place,
lower than the land all around it, among the oleander,

where people go when they know
that they need water, where we found him lying

by a wooden cross, looking toward us
as we walked—*looking*, I say. There is no other word for it.

# THE DEAD

We went back, but he wasn't there.
We went back, and it had become spring.

Cactuses were blooming. And his white head,
it wasn't there. Other bones, yes,

there were other bones,
there must have been, under the bushes,

under the shale, and Wendy said,
*The sheriff didn't get all of him—*

She dug in the shale until I said, *Stop.*
Then she stopped and rocked back on her heels.

We put red candles on the rocks.
And we left money, for his soul. We left pesos—

the dead can use pesos. We ate oranges
in the shade, and then we drove back

to the city. We slept all evening
in the city, and woke when it was dark.

II.

Recovered Remains 1-80, Arizona-Mexico border, Fiscal Year 2009-2010, as compiled by Coalición de Derechos Humanos, county medical examiners, and Consular Offices

| # | Name | Sex | Age | Country | Date Discovered | Location Discovered | Cause of Death |
|---|------|-----|-----|---------|-----------------|---------------------|----------------|
| 1 | Andres Arroyos-Olivas | M | 18 | Unknown | 10/4/2009 | St. David (Cochise County) | Motor vehicle accident-driver |
| 2 | Unknown | M | Unk | Unknown | 10/6/2009 | Benson (Cochise County) | Exposure |
| 3 | Unknown | | Unk | Unknown | 10/9/2009 | Dirt road in Little Tucson | Undetermined |
| 4 | Unknown | | Unk | Unknown | 10/15/2009 | N 32 31.093  W 112 60.852 | Undetermined |
| 5 | Unknown | | Unk | Unknown | 10/16/2009 | N 31 35.975  W 111 49.288 | Undetermined |
| 6 | Unknown | M | Unk | Unknown | 10/19/2009 | N 31 56.528  W 112 44.930 | Undetermined-skeletal remains |
| 7 | Unknown | M | Unk | Unknown | 10/20/2009 | N 31 52.345  W 112 44.930 | Undetermined-skeletal remains |
| 8 | Unknown | M | Unk | Unknown | 10/21/2009 | Sierra Vista (Cochise County) | Exposure |
| 9 | Unknown | | Unk | Unknown | 10/24/2009 | 10 miles west of SR 286, MP 31 | Undetermined |
| 10 | Unknown | | Unk | Unknown | 10/26/2009 | 2.5 miles west of Crowhang Village | Undetermined |
| 11 | Unknown | F | Unk | Unknown | 10/26/2009 | Portal, AZ (Cochise County) | Exposure |
| 12 | Unknown | | Unk | Unknown | 10/28/2009 | N 32 06.677  W 111 35.975 | Undetermined-skeletal remains |
| 13 | Unknown | | Unk | Unknown | 11/1/2009 | N 31 47.925  W 111 07.322 | Undetermined |
| 14 | Mario Rivera-Rivera | M | 57 | México | 11/2/2009 | N 31 55.798  W 112 58.842 | Gunshot wound of the head |
| 15 | Unknown | | Unk | Unknown | 11/3/2009 | 5 miles east of North Komelic Village | Undetermined-skeletal remains |
| 16 | Unknown | | Unk | Unknown | 11/3/2009 | 5 miles east of North Komelic Village | Undetermined-skeletal remains |
| 17 | Unknown | F | Unk | Unknown | 11/4/2009 | N 32 48.201  W 112 09.152 | Undetermined (mummified, partially skeletonized remains) |
| 18 | Panchi Cosme-Avelino | M | 37 | Unknown | 11/10/2009 | Bisbee, AZ (Cochise County) | Motor vehicle accident-Pedestrian |
| 19 | Alfredo Cruz Tienda | M | Unk | Unknown | 11/10/2009 | Storey Road, west of Sunshine | Blunt impact to head and torso with multiple severe internal injuries |
| 20 | Ricardo de la Cruz Cruz | M | 49 | México | 11/10/2009 | Storey Road, west of Sunshine | Blunt impact to head and torso with multiple severe internal injuries |
| 21 | Jorge Islas Montiel | | | Unknown | 11/11/2009 | 1 mile west of Aqua Fria wash on Forest | Undetermined (decomposed, partially skeletonized remains) |

| | | | | | | | |
|---|---|---|---|---|---|---|---|
| 22 | Unknown | F | Unk | Unknown | 11/12/2009 | N 31 69.3017 W 110 98.2633 | Undetermined-skeletal remains |
| 23 | Unknown | | Unk | Unknown | 11/18/2009 | N 31 57.518 W 111 8.836 | Undetermined-skeletal remains |
| 24 | Unknown | M | Unk | Unknown | 11/27/2009 | N 31 59.833 W 111 44.246 | Undetermined |
| 25 | Jesus Ricardo Llanes-Robles | M | 29 | Unknown | 11/27/2009 | N 30 50.3574 W 111 10.7203 | Gunshot wounds to extremities with perforation of vascular structures |
| 26 | Unknown | M | Unk | Unknown | 11/28/2009 | N 32 02/091 W 112 04.696 | Undetermined |
| 27 | Unknown | | Unk | Unknown | 11/29/2009 | N 32 00.899 W 111 21.384 | Undetermined |
| 28 | Unknown | M | Unk | Unknown | 11/29/2009 | Unknown | Undetermined |
| 29 | Unknown | M | Unk | Unknown | 12/1/2009 | N 32 12.729 W 111 54.835 | Undetermined-skeletal remains |
| 30 | Luis Armando Castanon Morales | M | 35 | Unknown | 12/1/2009 | N 32 12.729 W 111 54.835 | Undetermined-skeletal remains |
| 31 | Unknown | M | Unk | Unknown | 12/1/2009 | N 32 12.729 W 111 54.835 | Undetermined-skeletal remains |
| 32 | David Morales Esparza | M | 44 | Unknown | 12/1/2009 | N 32 12.729 W 111 54.835 | Undetermined-skeletal remains |
| 33 | Lusio Palma Vizcarra | M | 25 | México | 12/3/2009 | Cortel and Wiltbank Roads | Blunt force injuries of head |
| 34 | Octavio Lopes Ruelas | M | 38 | México | 12/3/2009 | N 31 43.595 W 110 58.027 2.5 miles WE | Multiple gunshot wounds |
| 35 | Byron Rene Guerra Alarcon | M | 31 | Unknown | 12/4/2009 | N 32 19.967 W 112 10.751 Santa Rosa Village | Dehydration |
| 36 | Unknown | M | Unk | Unknown | 12/7/2009 | 0.4 miles south of MP 108, SR 86 | Undetermined |
| 37 | Unknown | M | Unk | Unknown | 12/10/2009 | Federal Route 34, 5 miles west of MP | Undetermined-skeletal remains |
| 38 | Unknown | | Unk | Unknown | 12/13/2009 | N 32 44.8555 W 111 75.492 | Undetermined-skeletal remains |
| 39 | Unknown | M | Unk | Unknown | 12/13/2009 | N 31 42.699 W 111 05.597 | Undetermined-skeletal remains |
| 40 | Unknown | M | Unk | Unknown | 12/16/2009 | White House Canyon Road, MP 2 | Undetermined-skeletal remains |
| 41 | Unknown | | Unk | Unknown | 12/18/2009 | N 31 8844 W 111 .4851 | Undetermined |
| 42 | Jose Juan Perez Camarillo | M | 28 | México | 12/19/2009 | 1.3 miles south of Federal Route 2 | Hyperthermia |
| 43 | Eleuterio Bautista-Romero | M | 28 | Unknown | 12/27/2009 | N 31 53.129 W 110 33.306 | Probable hypothermia |
| 44 | Unknown | M | Unk | Unknown | 12/29/2009 | Canal Gate B-5, Stanfield Foad and I-8 | Drowning |
| 45 | Agustin Gutierrez Ortis | M | 33 | Unknown | 1/2/2010 | N 32 26.318 W 111 37.612 | Undetermined-skeletal remains |
| 46 | Unknown | M | Unk | Unknown | 1/3/2010 | 3 miles southwest of Gu Vo Cemetery | Undetermined-skeletal remains |
| 47 | Jorge Solis | M | 28 | Unknown | 1/4/2010 | Douglas, AZ (Cochise County) | Gunshot wound |
| 48 | Miguel Rivera-Acosta | M | 32 | Unknown | 1/7/2010 | Douglas, AZ (Cochise County) | Exposure |
| 49 | Rafael Rivera-Vera | M | 22 | Unknown | 1/8/2010 | Douglas, AZ (Cochise County) | Motor vehicle accident |
| 50 | Luis Alonso Acosta Barreras | M | 29 | Unknown | 1/8/2010 | N 31 32.967 W 111 43.017 | Undetermined-skeletal remains |

| | | | | | | | |
|---|---|---|---|---|---|---|---|
| 51 | Unknown | M | Unk | Unknown | 1/13/2010 | N 31 42.255  W 112 14.813 | Undetermined- skeletal remains |
| 52 | Edith Carballo-Paredes | F | 25 | Unknown | 1/15/2010 | South Mission Road, MP 14 | Multiple blunt force injuries |
| 53 | Cristian Alfredo Cruz-Munguia | M | 21 | Unknown | 1/15/2010 | 6000 West Caterpillar Trail | Probable hypothermia |
| 54 | Juan Gabriel Santos Ramirez | M | 33 | Unknown | 1/15/2010 | Baboquivari Mountains | Probable hypothermia |
| 55 | Salvador Carbajal-Santos | M | 35 | México | 1/19/2010 | N 31 19.59  W 110 57.14 | Pending |
| 56 | Walter Odir Figueroa-Serrano | M | 33 | Unknown | 1/22/2010 | 8220 South Marsteller Road | Pending |
| 57 | Unknown | | Unk | Unknown | 1/23/2010 | N 31 81.069  W 111 50.194 | Undetermined- skeletal remains |
| 58 | Unknown | M | Unk | Unknown | 1/25/2010 | N 31 54.156  W 111 14.435 | Pending |
| 59 | Enrique Zapata-Sanudo | M | 47 | Unknown | 1/25/2010 | N 32 35.570  W 111 78.540 | Hypothermia |
| 60 | Teodoro Salcedo-Villa | M | 47 | Unknown | 1/27/2010 | N 31 53.218  W 111 29.455 | Probable hypothermia |
| 61 | Unknown | | Unk | Unknown | 1/30/2010 | N 38 48.474  W 110 58.587 | Undetermined |
| 62 | Unknown | M | Unk | Unknown | 1/31/2010 | 1 mile east of port of entry N 31 87.644 | Unknown |
| 63 | Unknown | M | Unk | Unknown | 2/1/2010 | Unknown | Probable hypothermia |
| 64 | Manuel Garcia-Pastana | M | 40 | Unknown | 2/1/2010 | Douglas, AZ (Cochise County) | Exposure |
| 65 | Bulmario Cruz Mejia | M | 31 | Unknown | 2/2/2010 | Unknown | Probable hypothermia |
| 66 | Saul Martinez del Villar | M | Unk | Unknown | 2/4/2010 | 1 miles south of 9322 South Carol Lane | Probable hypothermia |
| 67 | Felix Raymundo Escalante-Aguirre | M | 41 | México | 2/5/2010 | N 31 34.010  W 110 71.515 Forest Service Road 4719 | Probable hypothermia |
| 68 | Unknown | M | Unk | Unknown | 2/6/2010 | N 31 53.789  W 111 22.390 | Undetermined |
| 69 | Unknown | F | Unk | Unknown | 2/8/2010 | Sierra Vista (Cochise County) | Exposure |
| 70 | Unknown | F | Unk | Unknown | 2/8/2010 | St. David (Cochise County) | Pending |
| 71 | Unknown | F | Unk | Unknown | 2/8/2010 | Fort Huachuca (Cochise County) | Exposure |
| 72 | Unknown | | Unk | Unknown | 2/8/2010 | 13241 West Orange Grove Road | Gunshot wound of the head |
| 73 | Unknown | M | Unk | Unknown | 2/9/2010 | N 31 26.997  W 111 12.830 | Undetermined |
| 74 | Erik Ezequias Morales-Roblero | M | 19 | Unknown | 2/11/2010 | ½ mile west of Midway Road | Drowning |
| 75 | Unknown | | Unk | Unknown | 2/13/2010 | N 31 59.538  W 112 06.991 | Undetermined |
| 76 | Unknown | F | Unk | Unknown | 2/15/2010 | Palominas (Cochise County) | Undetermined |
| 77 | Unknown | F | Unk | Unknown | 2/16/2010 | Tombstone (Cochise County) | Exposure |
| 78 | Unknown | | Unk | Unknown | 2/16/2010 | N 32 29.623  W 111 83.702 | Undetermined |
| 79 | Unknown | M | Unk | Unknown | 2/18/2010 | N 32 32 36.356  W 111 39 36.1528 | Pending |
| 80 | Unknown | M | Unk | Unknown | 2/19/2010 | FR 286, MP 9 (Deadman's Pass) | Probable hypothermia |

# THE ORCHARD

There is an abandoned orchard on the road that runs east from the city to El Paso, and you can see by the old quarry the furrows that are green with clover now in March, pecans falling from the trees to the ground, their dark husks open and not open. The black and red birds fill the quiet with their singing.

We were quiet when we stood in the wash south of the orchard, and my friend said she was afraid the animals might come to the man we had found, if we left to climb the ridge and call the police. We didn't say, *He has already been here for months and months.* You could tell he was a god by the way his feet were broken.

# FEBRUARY

If it would be ennobling, I could say it was like this, Lupercalia,

or before Lupercalia, Februa, festival in Rome

before it was Rome, the word meaning *fever or rain*, festival

in which everything is washed in preparation for spring.

Like that, I could say, I showered every morning and again in the afternoon,

though we hadn't touched the man we found.  And I could say,

as in some ancient city, that there were reasons for the rules:

for letting the water run as hot as it would go,

and then, when I was done, for not looking at my body directly

but in a glance to one side when I stepped out of the tub,

steam on the long mirror clear in spots

from the wind that had blown the long window

by the medicine cabinet open, white curtains blowing out

and then back in again like the chest of a horse after it's stopped running.

The light came in differently at different times of day.

Then it was spring, too hot to shower much: when the washing stopped,

the rules stopped, and with them the idea that when

the sheriff lifted the man's skull into the bag it was so similar

to the gesture of cradling a sick person's head in your hands.

Then I couldn't remember if he'd been wearing a shirt,

then, for days at a time, why he mattered—

since he was never mine to have lost, since what I was washing

can only have been what I thought I thought.

# THE MATTRESS

*You think there's one story but there are many stories,* my friend was saying.
We were in North Carolina, walking by the river, and girls were sitting on
the rocks, passing cans of beer to one another, throwing smaller rocks into
the water: she meant that there were many ways to fall in love. I know she
meant to help. And I know it gets banal, after a while, this thing that keeps
turning back on itself—as today, at the end of September, the Arizona sky
blue over the mountains, when I pass a wash where homeless people sleep,
and see, at the bottom of the wash under the dirt, a quilted thing that might
have been covering a body, and I climb through the brush, and jump down
from the road into the wash, and with a branch try to lift the edge of it, hard
with weeks of grit and heat, try to lift it then, with my hands. And there's a
mattress spring, then a stick that might have been bone with skin on it, cars
passing on the road up in the sun.

# WHAT WAS MISSING (2)

Except Annie thinks that both of his shoes were there.

*They were side by side, as though he'd taken them off,*
she says, late at night in November—

only when she saw the other man, the one they found
two weeks ago, she thought at first he was very old,

and he wasn't old, he was young

so she might be wrong, since what I thought all this time
was that one was gone—

Wilson, the brand name
puffed out of the leather, the leather white,

the laces white, proof he'd come
from this world, since you can buy that kind of shoes here,

where there are birds on telephone wires, and a sky,
and a pomegranate tree outside in the morning

and my sister running fast into the yellow grass,
and a way to remember—

he'd just left it somewhere else, we had to look harder.

# OMISSION

She remembers the car, a silver Toyota with tan upholstery, outside the gray New England sky, October, and rain. Her father driving, her mother in the passenger seat, and rain slapping the windshield on 95 north. *Heart palpitations, collapsed*: was that a phrase thought up afterward, or had it actually been said, that afternoon, when the cross country coach she'd thought all fall of touching had, after the race, put one hand on her arm and told her to go home? In the backseat she was reading *Brave New World*, worn pages soft between her fingers. She'd heard it was a book to read if you wanted to be something, which must have also meant not to be dragged down by a current others seemed not to have the wherewithal to resist, so deep it was not visible except by the tracks it left, traces of vomit near the shower drain, handful of pills half-crushed in the coat pocket. The parking lot, she remembers, the white and pink brick of the hospital, the cold air when they got out of the car, and the elevator, the thin white blanket, narrow bed. But her sister's face, which must have been, as it was always then, puffy and smeared with foundation on her cheek, or her jaw, blood vessel burst, maybe, in one of her eyes: these did not seem to be there, or if they were, won't come clear, aren't palpable, as in, able to be touched, felt, handled, so as to be memorable.

# THE FIELD

The day after we found him it was cold and a steady rain was falling.
In the parking lot across the street from my house, I called her:

*We found a body,* I said, though I knew that wasn't right.
There must have been something of a man left in him

or the sheriff wouldn't have held each part of him
at arm's length, lifting, before he dropped it in the bag,

the skull, the bones of the feet, the jeans,
and with them dry leaves from where he'd been lying, dust,

pieces of shale. I got in the car and the rain was falling harder.
Her voice was quiet and she put her glasses on, moved one hand

to the switch for the wipers, then back to the wheel again.
I was telling the story and my voice was almost calm, her face,

looking straight ahead, smooth as though to soothe me.
*Over the ridge they couldn't get the bag up,*

*they threw it*—the noise she made then, of pity or comfort,
not a word but an exhalation,

like wind just starting in a field of wheat
somewhere in the middle of the country, wheat in her thin hands

on the wheel, wheat in her body where I was speaking
as a child might speak into a field and hear a rustle

that could be a bird taking off in the dark,
wings beating the stalks as it goes.

# HARVEST

But hadn't I planned for it to be exciting?

Wasn't it part of what I thought I would find, when I came?

That it would have the rush, the drama, of an episode of *Law and Order*,
the body, the unfolding sequence of hints and clues, the resolution in which
some landscape of a city opens out as it had in the beginning?

Hadn't I told my friend that since people are dying, I might find someone
who did?

Hadn't I come here anyway?

Hadn't I come here because?

Didn't I hold my faith in finding him as I would hold a prayer card in my
pocket, to be taken out, examined, written in a language I'd just begun to learn?

Wasn't it to have been a ladder?

Or a gate, made out of white boards and then boards from which the paint has been washed away, gate left unlatched so the wind could swing it open to a stand of trees where yellowing pears, about to drop, would sway in a wind that tastes of salt off the coast, and beyond the pears, along a path into the woods, the smell of wild grapes—ripe, and free for me to take?

# PACE

Someone has been deported who has HIV. He's beautiful:
black hair combed back from his face in waves,

dark red jeans hanging over his shoes. He sits in a plastic chair
and his face looks surprised, like maybe he didn't mean

to be crying. We can see the border from where we are beside him,
my friend and I, and since she's an RN, and calm, she leans over him:

his medicine's gone, and he won't go to the hospital
until he finds his friend who'd tried to cross with him—

another volunteer hands the man cold medicine, gel tablets
that are sea green, Christmas-color red.

Doesn't she know he has been shitting blood?
My friend is leaning over him, fighting with death.

Or maybe, as it has been said, it's God who wants to kill the man.
It's facing the two of them: only they can see its face,

its back the color of this afternoon, March light,
moon coming up as slow as it wants to.

# THE INSTRUMENT MAKER

Before he taught me about the glass he taught me about the copper,

how to cut the narrow pipe where he'd marked it,

different lengths for different notes,

then how to sand the edges down, make them dull and smooth,

line them up on the sawhorses. We'd wear two sweaters,

winter coats, masks to keep the dust out. It was cold in the basement:

it was January, outside, snow fell on top of snow—

twenty miles further to the coast, to Rockland, ten miles inland

to the farmhouse where the smell of hay came up from the barn

and into the kitchen, abstractions in the light from the gooseneck lamp

bent over the worktable, learning about the glass,

how to place a slender sheet under the drill, attach the diamond drill bit, lower the drill so it almost looked like it hadn't touched at all—

and then lift it, and then lower it again, to make a hole.

And the trick he taught me when I stayed late, how to make one cut

and then radial cuts around it, each an equal distance from the center,

and if they were in the right relationship to each other

the glass would break into a perfect circle, a single hole

exactly in the middle, like the meadow of snow, one tree

clean against it, that I passed on my way back.

# THE SPRING

Because Annie said, *Sometimes I imagine him as a child,*
which means she imagines a specific child,

because it rained tonight, this last night of August,

and the streets here don't have gutters, or drains,
so there's nothing they can do but hold it,

because the man we found won't tell me his true name,
and I don't know how to ask for it,

when I'm told that I should give him a name
my mind says no but my other mind is naming him,
*Elias*, variant form of Eli, meaning *Lord my God*—

though I'm scared I might lose track of this,
that the name is just a man on a hill pointing
to the one we found, the one

who wakes me at night so I won't forget
how his eyes were gone, how through that space

the earth could look out to the winter passing.

# RETURN

It's June, the last Saturday in June, when Wendy and I go back again to search the wash.

In April a doctor found another jaw there, and another jaw means another person.

Don't think, *thousands crossing every year, hundreds dying,* which they are, don't think, *this is never ending.*

There's a job to do, there's a plan, there's one man found by us, his bones the sheriff left behind: we'll bring the rest of his body back, and if there's another, bring that, too.

We park, walk up by the barbed wire fence and at the gate turn into the valley, toward the first ridge, the trees brown and low around us, the high crops of rock rising up after the steep downward walk, the dip between them where we'll cross into the second valley.

At the head of the wash, under the shade of mesquite, by the shrine we'd made in the rocks in March, we eat the apples we've brought, and the day is hot, but no hotter than another day in June as we walk together down the center of the wash, almost holding hands before we move apart, since it's a little bit like being children, climbing the sides where someone could slide down in the rain, looking for something white.

And when we find the trail not used anymore, the trace of a trail with a glass jar on it, it's like finding there are many worlds, and you can step in and out of them—in the end we go back to the center of the wash, to the spot where we found him, and crouch in the shale and dig with our hands, and I notice nearby a blue feather, faded almost to gray, and remember what I didn't say in February when Annie had climbed out to call the police and Wendy sat rocking, when I climbed out after Annie to get away from Wendy rocking, when I saw, at the steep part of the wash before it comes out on the land, a blue feather, the only thing, that day, made out of color, then the sheriff and his men arriving, how we showed them the way in from the road, and they held the man up before they put him in the bag, and Kevin said, *you don't have to watch* and I said, *but I want to*—

now Wendy is saying, *here's something*, and showing me the tooth she's found, then a thing shaped like a clavicle notch, like the spot in your throat where there are no bones.

And I kneel beside her and we put back what we have found, and cover it with dirt, and shale, and branches.

And I take off the blue bandana Annie gave me, and fold it on the branches.

III.

## Recovered Remains 81-161, Arizona-Mexico Border, Fiscal Year 2009-2010

| 81 | Ernestina de los Santos Cano | F | 27 | México | 2/21/2010 | Arivaca Road, MP 7 | Probable hypothermia |
|---|---|---|---|---|---|---|---|
| 82 | Antonio Ramirez Hernandez | M | 32 | México | 2/22/2010 | 1.2 miles north of the U.S./México border | Hypothermia |
| 83 | Unknown | | Unk | Unknown | 2/25/2010 | N 32 43.2  W 111 18.47 | Undetermined-skeletal remains |
| 84 | Unknown | | Unk | Unknown | 2/25/2010 | N 31 96.494  W 112 71.690 Ajo Mountain Loop Roa, Scenic Marker 21 | Undetermined |
| 85 | Unknown | M | Unk | Unknown | 2/25/2010 | Portal, AZ (Cochise County) | Exposure |
| 86 | Edwin Aroldo Estrada | M | 32 | Unknown | 2/26/2010 | Sierra Vista (Cochise County) | Complications of pneumonia |
| 87 | David Acosta-Ballardo | M | 52 | Unknown | 2/28/2010 | Federal Route 42, MP 18.6 | Multiple blunt force injuries |
| 88 | Eliazar Garcia-Valencia | M | 32 | Unknown | 3/1/2010 | N 31 72.047  W 111 59.663 | Blunt force injuries of head |
| 89 | Unknown | | Unk | Unknown | 3/5/2010 | 3 miles east of Cold Fields | Undetermined |
| 90 | Unknown | | Unk | Unknown | 3/11/2010 | N 31 92.950  W 112 88.745 | Undetermined |
| 91 | Unknown | | Unk | Unknown | 3/12/2010 | N 31 54.093  W 111 53.279 West of MP | Undetermined |
| 92 | Unknown | M | Unk | Unknown | 3/12/2010 | Unknown | Undetermined |
| 93 | Luna Abreu, Yomelina Altagracia | M | 32 | Unknown | 3/15/2010 | Sierra Vista (Cochise County) | Exposure |
| 94 | Unknown | M | Unk | Unknown | 3/16/2010 | N 31 39.692  W 110 28.893 | Probable hypothermia |
| 95 | Unknown | | Unk | Unknown | 3/19/2010 | 5.5 miles north of Mile Post 19 on Federal Route 35 | Undetermined |
| 96 | Ballardo Huerta Avila | M | 27 | Unknown | 3/28/2010 | N 31 55.584  W 112 06.873 | Undetermined |
| 97 | Unknown | | Unk | Unknown | 3/28/2010 | N 31 49.368  W 112 02.776 | Undetermined |
| 98 | Unknown | | Unk | Unknown | 3/29/2010 | N 31 44.792  W 112 03.022 | Undetermined |
| 99 | Unknown | M | Unk | Unknown | 4/2/2010 | Sierra Vista (Cochise County) | Exposure |
| 100 | Leobardo Aleman-Silva | M | 22 | Unknown | 4/7/2010 | I-10 MP 238 E/B Frontage Road | Probable drowning |
| 101 | Heriberto Aja Borbon | M | 45 | Unknown | 4/8/2010 | N 32 03.610  W 112 45.913 | Undetermined-skeletal remains |
| 102 | Unknown | | Unk | Unknown | 4/9/2010 | N 31 26.997  W 111 12.776 | Undetermined-skeletal remains |
| 103 | Unknown | M | Unk | Unknown | 4/10/2010 | N 31 50.877  W 111 17.268 | Undetermined (decomposed, partially skeletonized remains) |
| 104 | Unknown | F | Unk | Unknown | 4/10/2010 | N 31 51.557  W 112 10.077 | Undetermined-skeletal remains |
| 105 | Jose Luis Ixtlahuaca Utrera | M | 37 | Unknown | 4/17/2010 | N 31 37.640  W 111 22.366 | Probable dehydration |
| 106 | Ramon Lara-Lara | M | 25 | Unknown | 4/17/2010 | N 31 58.658  W 112 30.169 | Dehydration |

| | | | | | | |
|---|---|---|---|---|---|---|
| 107 | Bernaldino Perez Salas | M | 32 | Unknown | 4/19/2010 | N 31 37.646  W 110 47.250 | Coronary atherosclerosis |
| 108 | Unknown | M | Unk | Unknown | 4/26/2020 | 2.8 miles southeast of Federal Route 21 | Undetermined |
| 109 | Humberto Sanchez-Bouchan | M | Unk | Unknown | 4/26/2010 | N 31 33.090  W 111 37.946 | Coronary atherosclerosis |
| 110 | Elvira Brambila-Vallejo | F | 44 | Unknown | 4/27/2010 | N 32 55.155  W 111 42.391 | Peritonitis |
| 111 | Margarito Perez de Jesus | M | 36 | Unknown | 4/29/2010 | N 31 38.269  W 09.105 | Pending |
| 112 | Eduardo Trejo Martinez | M | 21 | Unknown | 4/30/2010 | N 31  41.453  W 111 40.935 | Pending |
| 113 | Unknown | | Unk | Unknown | 4/30/2010 | N 32 03.517  W 112 11.932 | Undetermined-skeletal remains |
| 114 | Unknown | | Unk | Unknown | 5/1/2010 | N 31 49.439  W 111 54.738 | Undetermined |
| 115 | Unknown | | Unk | Unknown | 5/1/2010 | N 31 49.439  W 111 54.738 | Undetermined |
| 116 | Unknown | F | Unk | Unknown | 5/3/2010 | 0.5 miles from HWY 86, MP 116 | Undetermined-skeletal remains |
| 117 | Rebeca Solorio-Estrada | F | 48 | Unknown | 5/5/2010 | N 31 53.153  W 111 27.755 | Probable hyperthermia |
| 118 | Jaime Emmanuel Hernandez Alvarez | M | 22 | Unknown | 5/10/2010 | State Route 61 (at end) | Mass envenomation |
| 119 | Unknown | M | Unk | Unknown | 5/10/2010 | State Route 286, MP 33- 75m | Undetermined-partial skeletal remains |
| 120 | Unknown | | Unk | Unknown | 5/12/2010 | N 31 27.603  W 111 01.736 | Undetermined |
| 121 | Mariano Hernandez Ruano | M | 39 | Unknown | 5/14/2010 | N 31 28.211  W 111 23.63333 | Blunt force head trauma |
| 122 | Raul Bernabe Ramirez Vergara | M | 43 | México | 5/18/2010 | N 32 11.349  W 111 53.082 | Probable hyperthermia |
| 123 | Jaime Jurado-Barajas | M | 21 | Unknown | 5/22/2010 | N 31 50.324  W 111 53.835 (Tapawa) | Environmental heat exposure |
| 124 | Unknown | M | Unk | Unknown | 5/22/2010 | N 32 26.375  W 112 03.425 (Sells) | Undetermined (mummified, partially skeletonized remains) |
| 125 | Unknown | | Unk | Unknown | 5/22/2010 | N 31 85.826  W 111 21.940 | Undetermined (incomplete skeletonized remains) |
| 126 | Oscar Manuel Tello Rodriguez | M | 33 | Unknown | 5/23/2010 | N 31 52.196  W 112 00.626 | Undetermined (partially skeletonized remains) |
| 127 | Unknown | M | Unk | Unknown | 5/24/2010 | Sierra Vista (Cochise County) | Pending |
| 128 | Martin Olguin-Lozoya | M | 28 | Unknown | 5/26/2010 | N 31 37.915  W 111 02.215 | Pending |
| 129 | Jose Martin Onesto Perez | M | 33 | Unknown | 5/28/2010 | N 31 59.358  W 111 59.645 | Pending |
| 130 | Unknown | M | Unk | Unknown | 5/29/2010 | N 32 08.675  W 111 52.798 | Hyperthermia |
| 131 | Maria Reyes Ramirez | F | Unk | Unknown | 6/3/2010 | Benson (Cochise County) | Motor vehicle accident |
| 132 | Maria Reyes Ramirez's fetus | | Unk | Unknown | 6/3/2010 | Benson (Cochise County) | Motor vehicle accident |

| 133 | Unknown | M | Unk | Unknown | 6/3/2010 | N 32 35.563  W 112 11.932 | Probable hyperthermia |
|-----|---------|---|-----|---------|----------|---------------------------|------------------------|
| 134 | Reymundo Valverde Pacheco | M | 45 | Unknown | 6/5/2010 | N 31 42.797  W 112 04.222 | Undetermined-skeletal remains |
| 135 | Unknown | M | Unk | Unknown | 6/5/2010 | N 31 40.085  W 111 43.584 | Undetermined-skeletal remains |
| 136 | David Mendieta Zamora | M | 27 | México | 6/6/2010 | White House Canyon Road, MP 3.5 | Probable hyperthermia |
| 137 | Osmar Robledo Patricio | M | 25 | Unknown | 6/7/2010 | N 32 79.02  W 112 16.333 (Antelope Peak) | Exsanguination |
| 138 | Amilcar Aguilar Najera | M | 21 | Unknown | 6/7/2010 | N 32 79.02  W 112 16.333 (Antelope Peak) | Gunshot wound of abdomen |
| 139 | Unknown | M | Unk | Unknown | 6/7/2010 | N 32 40.214  W 112 04.478 | Dehydration |
| 140 | Ruben Ortiz- Gerogana | M | 27 | México | 6/7/2010 | N 32 33.835  W 111 55.033 | Probable hyperthermia |
| 141 | Joel Lugo Bojorquez | M | 21 | Unknown | 6/8/2010 | N 32 44.937  W 112 12.857 | Probable hyperthermia |
| 142 | Alberto Donato Lopez | M | 40 | Unknown | 6/11/2010 | N 31 29.394  W 111 04.034 1.5 miles W | Undetermined |
| 143 | Unknown | M | Unk | Unknown | 6/11/2010 | N 32 17.818  W 111 22.904 | Probable hyperthermia |
| 144 | Unknown | F | Unk | Unknown | 6/15/2010 | McNeal (Cochise County) | Undetermined |
| 145 | Unknown | F | Unk | Unknown | 6/16/2010 | N 31 45.959  W 112 06.163 Tecolote Ranch | Probable hyperthermia |
| 146 | Wilmer Oswaldo Castillo Aguirre | | 17 | El Salvador | 6/19/2010 | N 31 59.971  W 112 18.333 Pisinimo | Probable hyperthermia |
| 147 | Manuel Vargas Zaldivar | M | Unk | Unknown | 6/22/2010 | 3 miles south of WHY 86, MP 101 | Hyperthermia |
| 148 | Unknown | F | Unk | Unknown | 6/23/2010 | N 31 44.11  W 112 10.173 | Probable hyperthermia |
| 149 | Filiberta Vasquez Garcia | F | 42 | Unknown | 6/24/2010 | N 31 53.427  W 111 42.290 (Arivaca) | Pending |
| 150 | Unknown | M | Unk | Unknown | 6/24/2010 | Benson (Cochise County) | Exposure |
| 151 | Unknown | | Unk | Unknown | 6/25/2010 | N 31 21.921  W 110 39.304 | Undetermined |
| 152 | Luis Alfonso Tatul Xitumul | M | Unk | Unknown | 6/26/2010 | 3655 South Kolb Road | Acute renal failure |
| 153 | Rey David Perez Vera | M | Unk | Unknown | 6/26/2010 | N 31 53.477  W 111 50.598 | Probable hyperthermia |
| 154 | Enemias Francisco Lopez Lopez | M | 28 | Unknown | 6/28/2010 | N 31 54.990  W 112 09.018 (Sells) | Probable hyperthermia |
| 155 | Unknown | M | Unk | Unknown | 6/29/2010 | N 32 39.277  W 112 08.396 | Probable hyperthermia |
| 156 | Unknown | F | Unk | Unknown | 6/30/10 | N 32 75.9018  W 111 42.4515 | Drowning |
| 157 | Alfredo Daboxtha-Daiel | M | Unk | Unknown | 7/1/2010 | N 31 51.561  W 111 56.905 | Probable hyperthermia |
| 158 | Nicolas Quintana Valenzuela | M | 28 | Unknown | 7/2/2010 | N 31 36.694  W 110 66.743 | Probable hyperthermia |
| 159 | Fatima Paulina Santos Borrero | F | 41 | Dominican Republic | 7/2/2010 | N 31 53.944  W 112 07.764 | Probable hyperthermia and dehydration |
| 160 | Unknown | F | Unk | Unknown | 7/2/2010 | N 31 55.417  W 112 09.094 | Dehydration and hyperthermia |
| 161 | Unknown | M | Unk | Unknown | 7/2/2010 | N 31 55.417  W 112 09.094 | Dehydration and hyperthermia |

# REST (2)

On the night she made me a sandwich, brought it to me in a paper bag

in the cold under the stars before we went in to hear the others read,

she told me that I got it wrong, the story about her,

in which, the way I'd written it, she was a child with other children,

alone with them by a lake for the summer, and young as they were

they'd not only stayed alive but also kept the same fire going

for months on end. *Anyway,* she said, *it's implausible,*

*what you wrote,* since actually she'd been a camp counselor,

almost an adult, and if there'd been a fire it didn't really burn that long,

or maybe it didn't matter the way I thought it mattered—

and maybe the point was she's a person, not a myth.

Maybe it's unfair to turn someone into myth,

but I thought those girls had made a deal with each other

to keep the fire going, the younger girls in charge

in the morning when it was strong, the older ones at night

when it started to die down. They did it by trading off,

is what I thought, passing the chore from one to the next like the baton

in a track relay when I was fifteen, outside the snow

coming down inaudibly and in the dry gym the only sound

the heat in my lungs until the last lap when I could pass it off

to whoever was fastest, then,

effortlessly, almost, since I knew she would win

and whatever mistakes I'd made, she would make up for them.

# REMAINDER

The idea being to go back to the canyon and fix up the shrine, and bring new candles, yellow mums, we go, though since it's October and eight months since we were last there I ask the others to remind me where to turn through the barbed wire fence, and Wendy takes her inhaler out at the steep part, since she's moved to Michigan since then, her lungs, on her short visit back, not acclimated to the air here. At the mouth of the wash where the rocks are white, Annie stays by the altar we'd built, and I go with Wendy down into the wash as we did before. The wooden cross we'd found by him, two sticks tied together with grass and string, is still there. And the red bowl Wendy brought last year to burn sage in, and a yellow candle someone else must have left, its glass container cracked—and placed next to the candle, I'm sure it was placed, a bone the size and shape of a shoulder blade, ridge of thicker bone at the top flaring out in two directions. *It's so light*, Wendy says, lifting it, putting it back down. Around us the wind picks up as it does near the ocean.

# THE HERON

An Egyptian king buried with a boat to travel in:

wasn't he like that in a way,
the man we found,

the dust like balm if balm were dry?

And like the king's boat, made to go down the river
to another world,

wasn't he left with what he'd need to travel more,
since what he had was after all

all he'd had to travel that far with?

Or a crocus, you could say he was like that,
the way he haunts like a bulb in the ground

haunts with what it is becoming,
or if not a crocus, if not a king,

anything that's ever been lost, hurt, discarded—

*you could compare him to anything,*
she said, *that's why he's so heavy.*

But that also means if you put him down

he stops being what he is.
Isn't *the honesty of things where they resist?*

And isn't he, then, more like this:
the heron I'd seen twice at the river this week,

on a rock in the water near where I was walking—

when I'd walk toward it, it would take off,
then land again a few feet away,

so Nathan says it must be sick,
since the healthy ones fly south,

to South Carolina. He lives there:

he's seen them coming in the fall, wide wings
the color of marshes. I thought the heron

had appeared for me,
and the problem was just that I couldn't read it.

But maybe he couldn't fly away fast enough,
from the half-frozen river,

from the branches extending. Not glass,
but the color of glass.

Or maybe he was wintering:

maybe he didn't need as much warmth as they said,
didn't need others like him there.

# USING IT

*Why don't you begin by telling me the story.*

Denver, on a bus into the city, to either side of the road the fields bare and wide, wire fences lining them in the wind. Still some snow on the grass, on the furrows. And over us, over the highway, a clear, light sky.

*Where did you find the body? Was there a trail?*

My friend saying, go have fun, telling me the way to a party a mile from the hotel, past the buildings with glass and steel panels. Inside, Christmas lights strung up on the rafters, red and green, then the white face of a woman, dark in the gap between her front teeth, cuff of her fake suede coat brushing my arm.

*What did you see first?*

Gold ring, name of her husband, her work in the Catskills. She said, *come over here so we can talk*, her hand on my knee when we sat down. I said, *yes it's hard sometimes*, I said, *in February we found a man who died.*

*Did he have a face?*

I said it so she'd keep her hand on my knee longer. She said, *you have sweet hands.*

*Was the body in parts, or how did you carry it?*

By the river in May where we said we'd meet, smell of water at night. She said, *your problem is you think too much.* Thinking: of who was using who, was using what.

# THE FAMILIAR

Home in December she takes the walk she always did,

behind the house, down the path to the stone wall in the woods,

one side of a rectangle of wall that marks

what had once been a pasture. The year has been warm;

the briars are still green at the edges of the wall, further in

the grove of pines, the oldest ones bare up to the top, their top branches

having taken all the sun. And it's quiet now as it was then,

when she followed her sister to where she knew she'd find her,

lying in the path, bleached hair in the dirt, not sleeping but vague

since she'd only taken enough of whatever it was to make her tired,

the rest of the pills in the pockets of her coat—

it was spring, March, the crocuses by the wall still closed

but cream-colored and purple, yellow and white,

bulbs the owners of the pasture must have planted, or a woman,

alone in a dress patterned with little yellow flowers—

at least, that's how she told the story, or thought but didn't say;

no need to say it then, her sister knew everything,

even when they didn't share the room with trundle beds,

one pulling out from the other like a drawer.

# AT TRUSTOM POND

*He wanted to know what he heard, not to get closer.*
—*Jack Gilbert*

Over the food my friend has made for my visit, fish, bread,
white wine the color of the August evening in Massachusetts,
he tells me that the poet is in an institution now,

an assisted living center in Southern California.
Who would have known how to describe this meal so that,
reading it, we could remember what bread is, and fish,

who wrote about vineyards and work in that remote place where,
despite years spent with beautiful women,
he'd gone to live alone—to write, maybe, the poems in which

the bodies of women are almost all the same, who said to me
on the cold night in Northampton after he read, voice
slipping already, faltering, mispronouncing a word that anyway

should have come after the one he read next—
when I brought the thin black book for him to sign
and asked him how to do what he was doing, *what do you mean,*

*signing books?*—turning to the next person then, eyes clouded

like he couldn't see us, and maybe wouldn't have wanted to if he could.
How that fall and into the winter the book rested

by the bed at my girlfriend's parents' house where we were staying,
November and the trees baring themselves in the yard
out to the road and the town where we'd both grown up,

the sky gray and then white for days, and geese flying south
at the wildlife refuge where we would go walking,
where she'd drop her voice to practice sounding like a boy.

Her hair was reddish in that light, and curling, thick sweater
over a sports bra to hide her breasts, piano player hands
on the railing at the salt pond, and the water there made blue,

deep blue, by the poet's lines, their insistence on living fully
and then on leaving the world further and further behind
as though from that distance he could see what he'd left.

# THE SHIRT

Two years after we found him, the length of time, I'd heard,
they hold the unidentified before they bury them,

I am bent over a computer screen with a man in a suit
who is showing me the database they use, how you can search

by *date found* and find the case number, the case. *And pictures,*
he says, clicking on the photographs of the clothes—

as though by looking hard I could go back,
to when we found him, and the minutes before that,

when we followed the trail that we found as we were walking it,
finding and walking so aligned I think we could have closed our eyes;

and looking now I know what I forgot, the blue-gray shirt
with the Henley neck, long sleeves, one wrist fraying.

# THE SPOOL

After a while you learn to notice where the mind begins to catch,
to grasp around a view or a thought, to tighten,

like thread around a spool, the spool in his pocket,

according to the website that I am reading again,
that lists the items found with him:

the scrap of paper rolled up in the center of the spool,
the phone number on it, no area code—

you learn, then, gently to unwind it, which feels like relief,
like that first night before they'd crossed

but were already in the desert, the guide,
who would have had a gun or at least a knife, telling them

to turn over what they had, maps, lists of phone numbers
and addresses in Chicago or Durham or Lafayette;

and he would have taken out the spool to be examined—

the guide would have glanced at it, would have then moved on—
his face showing no expression as he put it back.

# THE STUDIO


Two hours from Dublin, near this border with the north, rain every day

clears to passages of sun or at least to light

coming through clouds on the farmland around us, the rhododendron,

the gravel drive that runs past the rooms for the dancers, the printmaker,

down the hill to the lake, with paths to walk along.

The email that you wrote last night, to volunteers still there

and those of us who've left, to say you found the body of a man

near Gila Bend, is characteristically restrained, formal:

you don't talk in detail about the man, how he would have crossed the border

at night, walked for days before he got there—instead you just describe

the land where you found him, the desert west of Tucson

near the air force base, almost no trees or shade, just the heat, since it's May, though you don't say that either. And similarly,

when I write to say *I'm sorry that you're going through this*

I know I won't hear back, you're not looking for that, though you stayed for weeks

at the house where I lived that year, and though,

the morning after my friends and I found someone, helped to carry his remains

back to the road in a bag, you came into the kitchen

where we were making coffee, hugged my friend, then asked to know

the exact location, the waypoints, so you could put them on a map.

What I like is how here, in the morning, I can choose a small spoon

or a big spoon to use, a white and blue bowl with a pattern of vines

or of a man standing up with an oar in a boat. And I like the water on the lake,

not at all like the surface of the moon, but like silver

before someone found it and turned it into something to use,

or maybe before anyone heard of silver,

so looking at the lake you wouldn't think to describe it

in terms of something else. You could simply refer to it as water.

# CAIRNS

Look, there's nothing there anymore. They cleared it away, the right scapula, shoulder blade, identifiable by how the thicker part at the top gives way to a thinner, triangular plate.

*

Fireflies coming in through the open door, and everyone is getting up from their chairs, putting their light jackets on.

That afternoon the first drops of rain fell on the table where we were sitting, where a praying mantis was killing an ant, dragging it across the metalwork. *We don't have to watch this,* she said, brushing them both onto a sheet of paper, then onto the bricks on the ground.

*

One way to remember, I've heard, is to build cairns where the bones are, make them out of stones or whatever you have on hand, water bottles, granola bars, so when you go back with the sheriff you can find them, though no need for it this time since it was just the one bone to go get, in the same spot where we found it in October despite the coyotes, the months of winter rain.

*

Because it was visible on the trail where people are walking. Because the website said it was missing from his body. Because it might belong to someone else—

*

Though when we got there and he took the roll of black trash bags from the pocket of his uniform, ripped one off to use, I wanted to say it looked right where it was, there on the rocks, the delicate brown leaves—

Then we were at the top of the hill, before the drop down the last ridge to the car, and the bag the sheriff had was starting to rip, the edge of the bone starting to tear through; then he put it in another bag, which lasted.

# THANKSGIVING

I.

In the hot bedroom half a mile from the border

I opened David's Catullus, the last lines of number sixty-three,

women mutilating themselves before a god, red pen marks

translating the Latin: *Drive other people crazy. Drive other people mad.*

We'd just come from mountains that were green for the first time in months,

as happens here in August, and the sun was going down

over the cottonwoods, Border Patrol trucks parked on the hills

as we drove up Grand Avenue and turned on Crawford by the liquor store,

where teenage girls were standing, and where one,

in a pink tank top that looked like silk, lifted her right hand to her left shoulder,

as we passed, to pull up the strap that had been falling down.

*There could be poems in which he does not appear,*

my teacher said. She meant the man we found. She meant,

I think, *go back to the world again.* But there are things with holes in them—

like the stone foundation where a house had been, where my sister and I played

when we were children, a house that must have burned,

though we never discussed it. Wild geese taking off from the lake.

My sister taking off her clothes. It was cold, and I think she wanted to see

how far she could go without minding, as at the end of the day, from indoors,

it can look like it's already gotten dark, but if you've been outside all day

you know this is the bluest part, deer putting their faces to the ground

to eat at the beginning of winter. No one could tell me how they knew to do that.

Or the bald eagles coming back, why they came back

not in Maine's far north but central Maine,

along the coast where people live, where I worked one fall

at a farm, and where I lived, thirty miles from the farm,

with a woman who sometimes filled the house with lilacs in glass jars.

In the evening, when she broke the jars one by one against the kitchen wall,

smell of lilacs, smell of beer, her hands didn't shake,

since the moon came in from the field outside, since beyond the field

were pines, then another field, we were alone, we could be anything there—

In the morning she'd wake me, light coming in through the green glass bottle

by the window by the bed, and I'd watch through the window

as she'd go out to the field, unstringing the electric fencing

for the sheep we kept. Some days she'd bring in basil

I'd planted in the yard, and how can you tell the difference

between the smell of basil, the sound of her voice slurred though it was still morning,

and what the voice was saying, something about beauty, something about

what we'd be, those days in September.

Later she'd go into her room. If you put your ear to the door

you could almost hear a sound coming out, like ocean stored

in the curve of a shell, raincoat over the window

to keep out the light, the apple tree in the yard, its delicate branches,

in a certain light it appeared almost intact—

2.

In June, walking all week from Sásabe to Tucson with fifty others who'd
come because people are dying in this desert, people were dying as we
walked, I made a list of things I'd tried that spring in exchange for which the
man we found might not have died, such as not sleeping, such as lighting
candles at specific times, such as praying. And this walk, carrying a plywood
cross through the desert as the others did, each cross bearing in permanent
marker the name of someone lost, though most, like mine, said *desconocido*,
which means *unknown*.

If I tried hard enough, while I walked with the cross, I could begin to
pretend that in another minute he'd walk toward us, Elias. And then, surely,
he would walk past us, since what would I say if I saw him like that, light
catching in the thin grass west of the highway. A tattoo, maybe, on his left
shoulder, a name so faded to green that I couldn't read it, and neither could
he, since he just saw what it used to be and not what it was becoming,
something closer to the shape his mouth made of trying not to express pain,
at seventeen, when he rolled back the sleeve of his blue and white school
uniform and a man bent over him with a needle and ink. On the wall over
both of them Elias watched a page torn from a magazine, photograph of
apple trees in the orchards of Washington State, where a girl wore a ring the
man with the needle had given her.

73

3.

The phone call came the second week of September, a man named
Andrés, calling from Washington, calling to say his sister was missing, left
behind two weeks ago in the desert west of Tucson, from a small town in
Guatemala, twenty-two years old—

Sarah was the one who took the call.

Sarah, who'd turned to me last spring, her calm face, her voice saying, *I
want you to know, the doctor went out to where you found the man, she found
other bones, she thinks they're from another body*—who'd said, weeks before
that, there's no space in ordinary life for grief, which is what people say,
only her face was a calm I wanted to put on, her long arm around me in
her green windbreaker.

In September, after she took the call, I stood with her in the gravel parking lot.

The afternoon sun came down around us, and we discussed going that day
or the next to look, though we didn't say the girl's name was *Santa* which
means *saint*, we weren't saying it had been two weeks already, we weren't
asking *at what point do you lose your name*—what Sarah said was, *let's go in
the morning.*

So in the morning we drove out to Ironwood, the others who had come to help following in the jeep behind us, to Nation land west of 86, the place Andrés had described, which was also the place Sarah had found the other girl, who'd come from the same town Santa came from, who'd been coming, in a pink sweatshirt, to surprise her fiancé in Oregon.

He'd called and asked Sarah to look, so she did, and she found the girl in Ironwood, in a shallow dip of sand under a tree.

*She has very long hair*, the fiancé had said, and *she did*, Sarah was saying, *she did have long hair.*

Then we were walking under the power lines, looking for a trail on the land running flat and hard to the mountains west of us, past the thin dirt roads rutted next to mobile homes rotting out, the dust of their walls held together with formaldehyde, but only just.

Imagine living in a place like that, the windows like windows a child would draw, the child watching you get up every morning, prepare meals out of habit, as people who live in shadows must sometimes touch their foreheads out of habit, to make sure they are still there, and later their grandchildren notice it, one hand like a flicker at the forehead.

4.

There's no secret to this. You look for a trail and then follow it,

though you have to know what to look for, and then try to not lose track of it,

when the sun, in the middle of the day,

begins to make things move around, when everything begins

to look like a trail, and the wind and even your own steps might be voices.

I wanted to ask Sarah if you get used to it, after a while,

the backpacks left under the trees in the wash. The empty gallon jugs.

Cotton shirts hung in mesquite trees, the fabric getting so soft and thin

you could almost see through it if you were to look.

But I didn't know how to ask, and we kept walking, two weeks since the girl was lost,

two weeks of Andrés sitting at some card table in Washington State while it rained in the orchards around him, praying, maybe—

then he was calling us from Washington and we were stopping,

we were standing in the thin shade of the power lines:

his sister had called, she was already detained, she was already

sent back to Guatemala, and Sarah said into the cell phone,

*thank God she's safe.*

                It's October. Out walking last night

after the first rain in weeks, I saw three nylon jack o' lanterns

swaying in the wind in someone's yard.

Fall here isn't like fall at home—

no lake, no geese taking off from the lake, no swallows in the trees

while my sister gets thinner. Coming up to Annie's house

last night after the rain, I opened the screen door without knocking,

washed glasses in the kitchen, waited for her to come back from the desert.

They'd found another man who died.

*Today wasn't like before,* she said. *Today I felt strong, I knew what to do,*

her voice getting high and thin in the night.

And I did what I knew how to do, though I didn't know I'd learned it,

brought sheets out of the closet, made a bed for her on the couch on the back porch,

pulled a mattress close and lay down on it.

After a while she lay down, too. And after a while I turned off the light,

left the two white vigil candles burning. Then I pulled a blanket over her,

which is what they'd done for the man they found that morning.

5.

I saw them when I got there at first light, the eagles, in the stand of pines

at the foot of a hill, settling into the shape of a crown in the branches.
I'd left when it was still dark, I'd scraped frost off the windshield,

driven out past the blueberry fields toward the farm
to work with the others, killing the turkeys John had raised.

The week before Thanksgiving. We pulled rubber gloves over our coats,

used our hands to break the ice in the tubs in the driveway,
where we'd put the birds we'd killed the day before—

*you've got to stop the heat fast*, John said, *or they'll go bad*—

it was up to us if they went bad or not. We pulled the feathers
out with knives, gutted them, bagged them,

weighed them in the shop. And when our hands got too cold

to hold the knives, we beat them on our legs and started again,
though later we'd wake and find they'd gone numb while we slept.

We worked until there was no more light. And before we drove home

in the freezing dark, the rain turning slowly to snow in the road,
we swept what was left, what we didn't need,

down the drain in the center of the floor in the shop,

so it ran to the trees where the eagles were waiting
for the river running toward them.

6.

*Strung out behind one who bolts like an unbroken ox*

Catullus writes. *Where did I imagine I'd find you?*

Though maybe, after so much practice, it starts to become clear—

not the way his face was not a face, the man we found,

but how, at the end of the walk through the desert in June,

we came down from the West into the city, to a park,

and people were waiting for us, clapping. And then it was time

to put the crosses down, lean them

together against a tree, and mine went with them.

Recovered Remains 162-253, Arizona-Mexico Border, Fiscal Year 2009-2010

| | | | | | | | |
|---|---|---|---|---|---|---|---|
| 162 | Orlando Antonio Lopez Salinas | M | 35 | Unknown | 7/2/2010 | N 31 55.417  W 112 09.094 | Dehydration and hyperthermia |
| 163 | Unknown | M | Unk | Unknown | 7/3/2010 | N 32 12.158  W 111 54.963 | Undetermined-skeletal remains |
| 164 | Unknown | M | Unk | Unknown | 7/4/2010 | N 32 00.053  W 111 44.145 | Undetermined-skeletal remains |
| 165 | Unknown | M | Unk | Unknown | 7/4/2010 | 4.5 miles east of Federal Rote 21 | Probable hyperthermia |
| 166 | Gregorio Soriano Gonzalez | M | 39 | Unknown | 7/5/2010 | 8 miles north of Federal Route 30, MP 8 | Probable hyperthermia |
| 167 | Patricio Aki Alvarez | M | 19 | Unknown | 7/5/2010 | 6.6 miles north of San Pedro Village | Unknown |
| 168 | Unknown | M | Unk | Unknown | 7/5/2010 | Elfrida (Cochise County) | Exposure |
| 169 | Unknown | M | Unk | Unknown | 7/6/2010 | N 31 59.463  W 112 14.925 Pisinimo Village | Undetermined |
| 170 | Unknown | M | Unk | Unknown | 7/6/2010 | N 32 02.467  W 112 09.161 Pisinimo Village | Undetermined |
| 171 | Unknown | M | Unk | Unknown | 7/8/2010 | N 31 46.252  W 111 42.270 | Probable hyperthermia |
| 172 | Unknown | M | Unk | Unknown | 7/8/2010 | 3 miles west of Route 19, MP 16 | Probable hyperthermia |
| 173 | Sergio Franco Ramos | M | Unk | Unknown | 7/8/2010 | N 31 45.611  W 112 04.058 Cowlic Village | Probable hyperthermia |
| 174 | Unknown | | Unk | Unknown | 7/9/2010 | N 32 02.190  W 112 18.744 | Undetermined-skeletal remains |
| 175 | Maria Julieta Lorenzo-Garcia | F | 23 | México | 7/9/2010 | N 31 44.170  W 112 13.299 | Complications of hyperthermia |
| 176 | Unknown | F | Unk | Unknown | 7/9/2010 | N 31 58.389  W 112 21.750 | Probable hyperthermia |
| 177 | Unknown | M | Unk | Unknown | 7/11/2010 | N 31 47.602  W 112 26.025  Papago Farms | Undetermined-skeletal remains |
| 178 | Unknown | M | Unk | Unknown | 7/9/2010 | Benson (Cochise County) | Exposure |
| 179 | Fidel Vargas Parra | M | 17 | Unknown | 7/11/2010 | N 31 46.570  W 112 2.388  (Pisinimo) | Probable hyperthermia |
| 180 | Unknown | M | Unk | Unknown | 7/11/2010 | N 32 13.009  W 111 57.209 Ak Chin | Probable hyperthermia |
| 181 | Unknown | M | Unk | Unknown | 7/11/2010 | N 32 13.444  W 111 57.383 | Probable hyperthermia |
| 182 | Unknown | | Unk | Unknown | 7/11/2010 | N 31 57.982  W 111 17.313 Three Points | Undetermined-skeletal remains |
| 183 | Unknown | M | Unk | Unknown | 7/11/2010 | 8620 North Mesquite Oasis Road | Undetermined |
| 184 | Unknown | M | Unk | Unknown | 7/12/2010 | N 32 35.815  W 113 10.6983 | Probable hyperthermia |
| 185 | Unknown | F | Unk | Unknown | 7/12/2010 | N 32 07.394  W 112 12.891 | Undetermined (mummified, partially skeletonized remains) |
| 186 | Unknown | | Unk | Unknown | 7/12/2010 | N 32 01.025  W 112 09.909 | Undetermined (partially skeletonized |

| | | | | | | | remains) |
|---|---|---|---|---|---|---|---|
| 187 | Unknown | | Unk | Unknown | 7/12/2010 | N 32 10.330  W 112  09.994 | Undetermined |
| 188 | Unknown | | Unk | Unknown | 7/13/2010 | N 32 01.100  W 112 09.806 | Undetermined (partially skeletonized remains) |
| 189 | Unknown | M | Unk | Unknown | 7/13/2010 | N 31 47.169  W 111 51.759 | Probable hyperthermia |
| 190 | Unknown | M | Unk | Unknown | 7/14/2010 | N 31 36.42  W 111 54.61 | Probable hyperthermia |
| 191 | Unknown | M | Unk | Unknown | 7/15/2010 | N 31 55.233  W 112 10.667  Big Fields Village | Undetermined |
| 192 | Jose Rodriguez Altamirano | M | 37 | Unknown | 7/15/2010 | N 31 48.330  W 111 53.575 | Probable hyperthermia |
| 193 | Unknown | F | Unk | Unknown | 7/15/2010 | N 31 51.515  W 112 10.706 | Probable hyperthermia |
| 194 | Unknown | M | Unk | Unknown | 7/15/2010 | N 35 35.978  E 49 57.20 | Undetermined |
| 195 | Omar Velasquez Luna | M | 25 | Unknown | 7/15/2010 | N 31 06.862  W 112 19.451 | Probable hyperthermia |
| 196 | Unknown | F | Unk | Unknown | 7/15/2010 | State Route 86, north of MP 121.5 | Probable hyperthermia |
| 197 | Unknown | M | Unk | Unknown | 7/15/2010 | N 32 19.348  W 112 22.712  Vaya Chin Village | Undetermined |
| 198 | Jessie Daniel Palma Valenzuela | M | 29 | México | 7/17/2010 | N 31 86.519  W 112 76.180 | Probable hyperthermia |
| 199 | Ramon Alejandro Mendoza Alcaraz | M | 23 | México | 7/18/2010 | N 31 20.142  W 110 46.697 | Probable hyperthermia |
| 200 | Unknown | M | Unk | Unknown | 7/20/2010 | Federal Route 20, MP 1 | Probable hyperthermia |
| 201 | Unknown | M | Unk | Unknown | 7/20/2010 | Federal Route 19, MP 10 | Undetermined |
| 202 | Unknown | M | Unk | Unknown | 7/20/2010 | N 32 08.760  W 112 57.105 (Ajo) | Probable hyperthermia |
| 203 | Unknown | M | Unk | Unknown | 7/20/2010 | N 31 39.281  W 111 59.416 (ITAC) | Undetermined |
| 204 | Unknown | M | Unk | Unknown | 7/22/2010 | N 32 32.842  W 112 09.068 Santa Rosa Village | Undetermined (mummified, partially skeletonized remains) |
| 205 | Gilberto Garcia Guzman | M | 33 | México | 7/22/2010 | 4 miles south of I-8, MP 147 | Hyperthermia |
| 206 | Moises Bautista Anguiano | M | 41 | México | 7/24/2010 | N 31 716.18  W 112 284.73 | Pending |
| 207 | Diego Gutierrez | M | 25 | México | 7/25/2010 | 4 miles east of Route 21, MP 15 | Hyperthermia |
| 208 | Unknown | M | Unk | Unknown | 7/25/2010 | N 32 28.452  W 111 56.393 | Probable hyperthermia and dehydration |
| 209 | Unknown | M | Unk | Unknown | 7/25/2010 | N 32 28.456  W 111 56.364 | Hanging |
| 210 | Unknown | M | Unk | Unknown | 7/25/2010 | N 32 28.363  W 111 56.339 | Probable hyperthermia and dehydration |
| 211 | Jose Francisco Lidas Cendo | M | 28 | Unknown | 7/25/2010 | 1 mile southeast of FSR 799 and FSR 58 | Probable hyperthermia |

| | | | | | | | and dehydration |
|---|---|---|---|---|---|---|---|
| 212 | Jorge Romero Hernandez | M | 29 | Unknown | 7/26/2010 | N 32 39.406 W 112 04.387 | Probable hyperthermia |
| 213 | Unknown | M | Unk | Unknown | 7/26/2010 | N 32 00.913 W 112 57.694 | Probable hyperthermia |
| 214 | Unknown | M | Unk | Unknown | 7/27/2010 | N 32 02.089 W 112 72.685 | Pending |
| 215 | Unknown | M | Unk | Unknown | 7/28/2010 | N 31 48.153 W 111 56.593 | Environmental heat exposure |
| 216 | Israel Bueno Sanchez | M | 26 | Unknown | 7/28/2010 | Federal Route 15 and MP 38.5 | Environmental heat exposure |
| 217 | Unknown | | Unk | Unknown | 7/29/2010 | N 32 10.213 W 111 21.703 | Undetermined-skeletal remains |
| 218 | Unknown | | Unk | Unknown | 8/1/2010 | N 32 03.824 112 12.494 | Undetermined (mummified, partially skeletonized remains) |
| 219 | Unknown | | Unk | Unknown | 8/1/2010 | N 32 03.818 W 112 12.509 | Undetermined (mummified, partially skeletonized remains) |
| 220 | Juan Santiz Lopez | M | 17 | Unknown | 8/3/2010 | Caminio Tierra and Antonio | Probable hyperthermia |
| 221 | Carlos Jose Sandres Venegas | M | Unk | Unknown | 8/3/2010 | N 31 55.987 W 110 33.947 | Perforated duodenal ulcer |
| 222 | Unknown | | Unk | Unknown | 8/8/2010 | N 32 11.399 W 111 21.911 (Garcia Strip) | Undetermined-skeletal remains |
| 223 | Unknown | M | Unk | Unknown | 8/8/2010 | N 32 49.614 W 112 02.042 | Undetermined |
| 224 | Unknown | F | Unk | Unknown | 8/10/2010 | N 32 17.062 W 111 36.295 | Undetermined |
| 225 | Unknown | M | Unk | Unknown | 8/10/2010 | N 32 10.1919 W 111 21.7576 | Undetermined |
| 226 | Unknown | F | Unk | Unknown | 8/11/2010 | N 32 47.481 W 112 03.257 | Hyperthermia |
| 227 | Unknown | M | Unk | Unknown | 8/13/2010 | N 32 04.688 W 111 45.308 | Hyperthermia |
| 228 | Unknown | M | Unk | Unknown | 8/15/2010 | N 32 24.223 W 112 41.380 | Undetermined-skeletal remains |
| 229 | Rigoberto Valdez Pacheco | M | 29 | Unknown | 8/14/2010 | N 32 16.631 W 112 52.987 | Undetermined (mummified remains) |
| 230 | Ascencion Quelchulpa Xicalhua | M | 29 | Unknown | 8/16/2010 | N 32 28.166 W 112 16.875 | Hyperthermia and dehydration |
| 231 | Unknown | | Unk | Unknown | 8/18/2010 | N 31 79.415 W 111 00.673 | Undetermined (partial skeletal remains) |
| 232 | Unknown | | Unk | Unknown | 8/18/2010 | N 31 34.104 W 111 08.245 | Undetermined (partial skeletal remains) |
| 233 | Unknown | | Unk | Unknown | 8/20/2010 | N 31 57.093 W 113 00.665 | Probable hyperthermia |
| 234 | Jesus Vicente Gutierrez Rico | M | Unk | Unknown | 8/21/2010 | State Route 85 and MP 79 | Probable hyperthermia |
| 235 | Unknown | | Unk | Unknown | 8/23/2010 | N 31 59.182 W 112 08.913 | Undetermined |
| 236 | Unknown | M | Unk | Unknown | 8/23/2010 | N 32 09.532 W 111 22.515 | Undetermined |

| | | | | | | | |
|---|---|---|---|---|---|---|---|
| 237 | Francisco Guadalupe Romero | M | 31 | México | 8/27/2010 | N 32 24.945  W 113 16.076 | Probable hyperthermia |
| 238 | Unknown | M | | Unknown | 8/28/2010 | N 32 11.891  W 111 56.290  Cababi Village | Undetermined-skeletal remains |
| 239 | Unknown | M | | Unknown | 8/28/2010 | N 32 11.891  W 111 56.290  Cababi Village | Undetermined-skeletal remains |
| 240 | Unknown | M | Unk | Unknown | 9/3/2010 | N 32 00.20  W 112 38.03 | Undetermined |
| 241 | Unknown | M | Unk | Unknown | 9/4/2010 | Unknown | Drowning |
| 242 | Unknown | M | Unk | Unknown | 9/5/2010 | N 31 41.575  W 111 59.044 | Undetermined |
| 243 | Unknown | | Unk | Unknown | 9/9/2010 | N 31 41.999  W 111 51.695 | Hyperthermia |
| 244 | Unknown | F | Unk | Unknown | 9/14/2010 | N 32 11.882  W 111 21.810 | Undetermined-skeletal remains |
| 245 | Unknown | M | Unk | Unknown | 9/16/2010 | State Route 86, MP 63 | Probable hyperthermia and dehydration |
| 246 | Unknown | M | Unk | Unknown | 9/17/2010 | N 32 0.789  W 112 21.793 | Undetermined-decomposed partially mummified remains |
| 247 | Unknown | M | Unk | Unknown | 9/17/2010 | N 32 25.708  W 111 33.913 | Environmental heat exposure |
| 248 | Unknown | | Unk | Unknown | 9/18/2010 | N 32 52.483  W 112 9.966 | Undetermined |
| 249 | Unknown | M | Unk | Unknown | 9/21/2010 | N 32 17.427  W 111 52.257 | Probable hyperthermia |
| 250 | Unknown | | Unk | Unknown | 9/27/2010 | N 32 10.162  W 111 28.183  San Pedro Village | Undetermined-skeletal remains |
| 251 | Unknown | F | Unk | Unknown | 9/28/2010 | N 32 07.432  W 112 12.906 | Undetermined (partial skeletal remains) |
| 252 | Unknown | M | Unk | Unknown | 9/28/2010 | N 32 07.432  W 112 12.906 | Undetermined (partial skeletal remains) |
| 253 | Unknown | F | Unk | Unknown | 9/28/2010 | N 31 81.970  W 112 38.174 | Environmental heat exposure |

Notes:

"Omission" takes its title from Elyse Fenton's poem "The Omission."

"The Heron" quotes these lines from Jorie Graham's "The Age of Reason":
"Isn't the / honesty/ of things where they/ resist?"

"Using It" takes its structure from "Sleet," by Alan Shapiro.

The appendix of recovered human remains on the Arizona-Mexico border, October 2009-September 2010, was taken from the Arizona Recovered Human Remains Project of Coalición de Derechos Humanos in Tucson, Arizona.

Acknowledgments:

Thank you to the editors of these journals, in which some of these poems first appeared, sometimes in different forms:

*Beloit Poetry Journal, Ecotone, The Missouri Review, New England Review, Poetry Northwest, Southern Humanities Review, The Southern Review,* and *Quarterly West.*

I am grateful to the MFA Program for Writers at Warren Wilson College, especially to Debra Allbery and to my teachers, James Longenbach, Ellen Bryant Voigt, Marianne Boruch, Mary Szybist, and Jennifer Grotz. I am deeply grateful, too, to the Rona Jaffe Foundation, the Tyrone Guthrie Centre, the Bread Loaf Writers' Conference, and the *Kenyon Review,* whose fellowships and support enabled the completion of this manuscript. All of my thanks to Martha Rhodes, Ryan Murphy, and Clarissa Long at Four Way Books for their belief in this book and their support at every step. I am grateful to Jenny Johnson, for her careful and ethical readings of drafts of these poems, to Patrick Donnelly, for his early and endless help, to Eleanor Wilner, for her generosity and example, to Jaquira Díaz, for her honesty and solidarity, and to Wendy Sampson, for her friendship.

Thank you to my partner Rebecca Seiferle, for her love, her clear seeing of these poems, and for being with me now and in what follows.

My work with No More Deaths / No Más Muertes informed the writing of this manuscript; I am indebted to the volunteers whose knowledge, vision, and integrity shaped the questions that these poems try to ask. I would also like to thank Coalición de Derechos Humanos in Tucson, Arizona, for their efforts to honor every life lost on the U.S./ Mexico border, and for their work to maintain accurate records of those who have been found. I am grateful, finally, to the many people who shared with me some part of their histories and what they endured in trying to cross. This book, partial as it is, belongs to those who know the experience fully.

Publication of this book was made possible by grants and donations. We are also grateful to those individuals who participated in our 2017 Build a Book Program. They are:

Anonymous (6), Evan Archer, Sally Ball, Jan Bender-Zanoni, Zeke Berman, Kristina Bicher, Laurel Blossom, Carol Blum, Betsy Bonner, Mary Brancaccio, Lee Briccetti, Deirdre Brill, Anthony Cappo, Carla & Steven Carlson, Caroline Carlson, Stephanie Chang, Tina Chang, Liza Charlesworth, Maxwell Dana, Machi Davis, Marjorie Deninger, Lukas Fauset, Monica Ferrell, Emily Flitter, Jennifer Franklin, Martha Webster & Robert Fuentes, Chuck Gillett, Dorothy Goldman, Dr. Lauri Grossman, Naomi Guttman & Jonathan Mead, Steven Haas, Mary Heilner, Hermann Hesse, Deming Holleran, Nathaniel Hutner, Janet Jackson, Christopher Kempf, David Lee, Jen Levitt, Howard Levy, Owen Lewis, Paul Lisicky, Sara London & Dean Albarelli, David Long, Katie Longofono, Cynthia Lowen, Ralph & Mary Ann Lowen, Donna Masini, Louise Mathias, Catherine McArthur, Nathan McClain, Gregory McDonald, Britt Melewski, Kamilah Moon, Carolyn Murdoch, Rebecca & Daniel Okrent, Tracey Orick, Zachary Pace, Gregory Pardlo, Allyson Paty, Marcia & Chris Pelletiere, Taylor Pitts, Eileen Pollack, Barbara Preminger, Kevin Prufer, Vinode Ramgopal, Martha Rhodes, Peter & Jill Schireson, Roni & Richard Schotter, Soraya Shalforoosh, Peggy Shinner, James Snyder & Krista Fragos, Megan Staffel, Alice St. Claire-Long, Robin Taylor, Marjorie & Lew Tesser, Boris Thomas, Judith Thurman, Susan Walton, Calvin Wei, Abby Wender, Bill Wenthe, Allison Benis White, Elizabeth Whittlesey, Hao Wu, Monica Youn, and Leah Zander.